keeping

the

bees

employed

keeping the bees employed

Poems

R.B. Morris

Rich Mountain Bound
Knoxville
Tennessee

Second edition 2020
by

Rich Mountain Bound

ISBN 978-0-615-39365-0

Library of Congress Control Number: 2010911911

for Karly

and Fela

Contents

Epilogue: *Prelude to a New Season*

keeping the bees employed

keeping the bees employed

Well, I'd hardly say I'm employed
And yet I'm making it
I got the girl, she likes to say
My girl likes to say
When it appears as though
I didn't get much else, you know?

Our world is so different so
Removed really from
All the cultural meanderings
We don't keep up

But we get by
Barely, it seems to us
But what do we know?
We do a lot of what we like I suppose
Compared to most folks
But then, what do they know?

Hey, I just came in here to finish this beer
I've really got to get some sleep
It's been a long day
Like a year ago this morning
When she said, write that down
'Keeping the bees employed'
When I said, we have to find some way
To pay for this honey

the middle step

There's a tear in the carpet on the
Middle step as you enter this
Apartment building
I noticed it the first day we came here
It was much smaller then
Now I've entered and left the building
Thousands of times in the few years
We've lived here
But never once have I stepped on it
I've watched others step on it
I've watched it tear a little more
As the days go by

On the sidewalk out front
There are a few cracks between
The door and the parking lot
I always try to avoid stepping on the cracks
Just an old habit I guess
An old superstition
Or what is it then?
A distraction
A way of thinking
Of moving through the world
Over sidewalks
Through time
From your childhood to here
The crack between
A small ritual
Regards to the world
To the mystery
My mother
Her burden
Her back?

Of course if I had to move fast
Like jumping out of the way
Of a swerving car
I wouldn't think twice
About stepping on a crack
I wouldn't think once
I'd jump like a flushed chicken
And think it bad fortune indeed
To stand on ceremony

boiled eggs and toast

What is it makes you decide
To boil a couple of eggs
Put a couple of pieces of bread
In the old toaster?
Hunger, yeah, but it's been a long time
Since I boiled an egg

Anyway I didn't let them boil quite long enough
They were a little soft inside
Which makes them hard to peel
One of them started running before
I could get all the shell off
It wasn't a lost cause but difficult
I don't like the idea of watching the clock
So as to boil an egg the right amount of time
Whatever that is, I've forgotten
It's a feel thing for me
Most everything is at this point I guess
And this time, the first time in months
I jumped the gun

And now I've eaten
I've walked the dog
Talked to the mathematician neighbor
On the way back in
And had another cup of coffee
What's left for a man to do in this life?

years ago

There's a fellow lives across the way
I see him walking every now and then
Don't know his name
But I know he works at the hospital
That's where I met him years ago
When I had an accident
I fell off a roof and hurt my back
Broke both my feet and one wrist
Only had my already bummed up
Left hand to do anything with
I was laid up quite awhile
He was in physical therapy
And worked with me a few days
After I could be helped out of bed
He lives by himself
Walks down to the store and back
Or just out and around a few
Blocks and returns
Sometimes he'll sit out front of
His building in the sun
And just relax
He'll throw up a hand
Or nod if we happen to pass
Only once did we really stop and talk
He asked how I was doing
Did I recover okay?
I said yeah it all came back
Though sometimes my ankle
Hurts like hell for no apparent reason
He just smiled and said yeah
And we passed on by
But he was there
When I was all cracked up

He helped me
It was his job
But he helped me
Got me back on my feet
Showed me some tricks
With the crutches
Told me I was a quick learner
Built up my confidence
It was just for a few days many years ago
And now he's just some guy
Whose name I don't remember
Living alone across the way
In an old apartment building like me
But I won't be forgetting him

the blinking world

I step outside
In the morning sun

With the dog
She has no leash

I lean on a telephone pole
While she sniffs around

A fellow walks by
The dog's friendly and walks

A ways with him
He looks down at her as he walks

And then over to me
Says, good morning

Good morning, I say
The dog trails with him

A few more steps
Then starts back

He glances down to see
If she's still following

And walks on probably a student
On the way to the university

The weight of the light of the blinking world
Blinking in all our eyes

istanbul

The phone rings. I check the number. Hey.

What are you doing?

Well, I'm trying to write (believe it or not). You know, it's an archaic exercise like push-ups. So what's up with you?

Oh god, I've got a deposition this morning with a mad doctor, malpractice.

Yeah?

Yeah, but I'm working a couple of hours after lunch and then I'm out of here. I'm gonna take the top down today take the long way home.

Sounds good.

Yeah I figure 10-15 more years of this and I'm retiring. I figure I'm on the back 9 now and anything I got left is a gift.

Yeah, I know what you mean.

I've got the year planned. Me and the judge
are going to Istanbul.

Oh? That sounds good.

You ought to come with us.

Yeah? Man I wish I could.

Come on, I'll foot your plane fare if you'll pay
the rest. We'll have a blast.

Sounds great, but I don't think I can get away.

Man, you got to plan your work and work
your plan.

Yeah I hear that.

Agh, there's the phone, gotta go.

Okay, see ya.

See ya, bye.

iowa

Had some business this weekend
Engagements in Iowa
Turned out quite well, thank you
Before I left she sewed up my jacket
The back of the shoulder seam
I had gotten used to it
And in fact sort of went with it
The old torn coat of the poet
But she sewed it up
And you know it was better
It helped hold me together
Out there in the cold and heady world
Of music and songwriters who
Carry themselves like poets
On their way to ruin

But that's nothing
A man might have his arm ripped off
Torn from the body and not to be sewed back
And have to turn and go again
No second thoughts
Get used to it

the bastards wouldn't let me on the rodeo team
because I didn't have a horse

I laughed for a long time
When she told me that
It felt like the funniest thing
I'd heard in years
That was when she was
In a small college in Kentucky
She said she really wanted
On that rodeo team
I don't know, just sounded funny
As hell to hear her say it

Now her dog's back here
With the ball in her mouth again
Wanting me to throw it
I guess I signed on for this course

the morning diamond

Fellow who's a writer told me
He didn't want to have any kind of conversation
In the morning before he sat down to write
Said it worked out okay because his wife
Worked at night, and she's a writer too
I could understand this

All part of keeping it simple
Keeping it direct
First things first
Maybe even before coffee
While your dreams are still a fog
And all your atoms are still a'swirl
And not solidified yet into whoever
You're supposed to be
Get it down then
You can come back later and figure it out
Whatever it's about

Fuck what it's about
That's highly overrated
What could it possibly be about?
It's all just coming out
Do you want to keep it in?
What's your ritual little buddha?
What do you give back to the gods?
What do they give you?
And what do you do with it?

I've been blessed with a blind eye
A club hand and a diamond cutter
I can't figure out how to use

little asia

Little Asia I call it
Just these few blocks
And this because of all
The foreign exchange students
And Asian families
Living in the married
Student apartments
Across the way
For years
I've watched them
Young couples walking
From here to the university
And back
With their books and briefcases
Their babies in baby carriages
The mothers and fathers
Pushing them up and down the hill
Staring off at the trees and sky
Walking slowly pausing
To gaze off even more absently
Innocent young families
Far from home trying
To get an education
In the states
They give the neighborhood
An exotic air
Like nowhere else in town
And I too stare off at the sky
And trees in some faraway city
Looking for the sea

dogs and people

People out walking their dogs
Big dogs little dogs
Black and white and brown dogs
Spotted dogs and striped dogs
All kinds of mixed breeds even thoroughbreds
Just like the people
No wonder they call dog man's best friend
We're all mixed breeds too
And the thoroughbreds are usually stupid
All the good sense and ability bred
Right out of them
That should tell us something
And most of us on a leash as well
Being led around by someone or something
And really haven't learned how
To clean up after ourselves either
We scratch at doors, curl up on couches
Wait to get our heads patted our bellies rubbed
Happy to see those we love come home
And howl with mortal fear at the sound
Of death careening at us
But chasing after it when we can
We spy the lovely shape across the street
She stands up on great hind legs
She walks she wags she's strutting
She breaks into a skip then does a little dance
Before hurrying on along

Make a bulldog bust his chain
An old boy on the railroad used to tell me
Make a bulldog bust his chain

the can man

The can man goes by ragged and black
A great bag over his shoulder
Full of aluminum cans and
Other assorted treasures
A scraggly patch of beard hiding
Most of his face
And a tortured old hat pulled
Low to his eyes
But those eyes will find you
He's steady in his walk but
With a long limp
Winding him sideways like a crab
Dragging half his world
Behind the other
Making the morning rounds
To the dumpsters and garbage cans
Sometimes he talks to himself
Arguing with someone who's not there
And you hear him coming
Before he walks by the window
Or when you go to your car
Or pass him on the street
If his gaze crosses yours
You'd think he cursed you point blank
For bringing it all down on him
Gawldom moollycooggin blushet
Goin dog cone fug
Dong no jagg goowl

I think they should let him give this
Speech to the assembled luminaries of the city
The fathers and mothers who grace
The great offices overlooking

The river and downtown
I think they should let him limp
To the gilded podium and unload
His mighty poetry upon them
For he is the greater man
His work is pure and selfless
He's the one cleans up the mess
The trash the waste the excess
Of a bloated culture
Spilling out into the streets
Come rain or shine he's there
He knows every crack
Every cloud every face
He sees right through you
To that other place where
We all are but can't quite admit
He holds the city together
He's the cog that makes it click
He's the glue
He's your better
A true volunteer

mockingbirds

You walk these charming and often
Broken old sidewalks
Streets with names like Laurel and Bridge
Highland and Forest Avenue
And you don't ever get out of earshot
Of a mockingbird's song before
Another one takes over
Singing you into their precinct
They rule the air
They own this ridge
This whole neighborhood
And very territorial these guys
They've got it all mapped out
You just have to hear it
You see that two tone flash
In a low sweep beneath the trees
Or in full declaration atop
A telephone pole

Come on in!
Come on in!
I see you!
I see you!
Do you see me?
I hear you!
Do you hear me?

An oral tradition
Handed down beak to beak
In an old town
An old neighborhood
Now they could tell a history
If you could only read the book

War, murder, debauchery
Love and splendor, a child's song
Yeah they've seen it all
Just listen

renee's morning coffee ritual

One morning Renee
The Palestinian lady who
Owns the Falafel Hut
Down the way
Told me that when I stir my coffee
I should spoon up
The little bubbles that circle
At the top and if
I can gather them all up
In one swoop of my spoon
And sip them down
She said it would bring me
Good luck with money
So now I try to do this daily

I can only imagine how
Bad things would be otherwise

An empty hand in the afternoon

Ah, it's not even afternoon
What's your taste
I want to demolish time
I'm sure that's part of it
Just trying to crawl out of my skin
And bless all their hearts
I don't think badly of them
Though sometimes they do bore me
With their pressing uselessness
Their busy work
And their lack of curiosity, passion, vision,
Charity, thankfulness, honesty, or talent

But, I'm here if you need me

let's talk

You wanted to be Poet
Great conduit of spectral voices rising
Purveyor of light creasing the modern night
Appalachian Rimbaud exploding new Zen
Fountain of *duende* refounding
The good wild earth and sense of wonder
Singer of stage and air waves
Master of street corner and saloon
Prince of the beggar's bash
Renowned of kings and queens
Secret liaison into parts unknown
Mapper of mind and heart
The final frontiers

Yes I wanted to be Poet
Desire of song and language
I was Poet
I wrote poetry spoke poetry sang poetry
Poetry for the people
Poetry for the great poets
Poetry for God and Nature
Poetry for no God no Nature
Poetry for the moment
Poetry for all time
Poetry in the traditions
Poetry that broke tradition
Poetry that was broke
Poetry that enriched the land
From which it sprang
Heightened language, as they say
A living language
A long play of words and sounds
Poetry

But it didn't much matter to anyone
Or do anyone much good
After awhile the media threw in
An extra adjective or two
The academics patted you on the back
People on the street might threaten
You with an obscure presumption
Or treat you with a vague respect
Possibly even buy you a beer
And this is good
But had nothing to do with the poetry itself
People may be pleased you do it
They might think it's a good thing
But they themselves don't connect
Directly to it
It's rarely their song to sing

So I say forget the fifty cent word
If not the whole broken lined enterprise
This endeavor that doesn't deliver
Doesn't enlighten or inform
Or heal or reveal
Doesn't bring mercy
Or significant communication
Let it go

Let's just talk

the deal

I got a woman and she got a dog
And that's my tribe
We have our friends
Down here in the fringe
We're extended family occasionally
But I got a woman and she got a dog
And that's the deal
We can't be found in the big picture
We're lost but easy enough to locate
If anyone's looking
I might not be in the book
And the IRS isn't much interested
But others will have a quick file
On who and where and how much I am
Should anyone need to know
And someone will know
Every phone call made overseas
Or local if need be
Every email sent out and received
Every message every text
Every letter opened
Or stray distraction
Every busty lust takes on ball team
Or vote hawks or doves
Or do you love Jesus?
Or who do you love?
Yes I'm here if they want me
They just don't want me
At least not for the moment
But if they did
I'd be eliminated in a minute
If such things were allowed
And believe me they are

forging the days

Two afternoons in a row here
In the sweltering heat of dog days
My sweetheart and I have taken
Siestas after our meager lunches
Normally she gardens 8 hours a day
Out in the 90 plus degree scorch
And high humidity cooking her brain
In the merciless ozone cancer rays
Then after a full shift comes home
For an hour or so
Before going to the university
To work as a blacksmith
For another 3 hours
In a sweaty furnace of forges
And fired steel that
She pounds with a hammer
Big enough to drive railroad spikes
Beating and tormenting metal
Into useful shapes
Now that's a hard day's work
By any hardcore blue collar
Working class hero standard
In whatever salt mines you got
But yesterday and today
They let her off early
Today being the hottest day of the year
And yesterday just as hot
With workers falling out as they are
All over the country
And dying in record numbers
The boss decided better
To let the crew off a little early
Than have them fall over dead

And fresh out of groceries
And the rent due
We made our tomato and mayo sandwiches
And ate happily with smiles
And promises to pull it
Together better soon and laid
Ourselves down on the bed
In front of the fan
And fell into a slumber
Of blown dreams and heat noise
From the street holding each other
As close as we could without
Adding to the smothering
Weight of sucked out air
And slept there
For the better part of an hour

Ah... the siesta, a fine and valuable tradition
Though one the gringo is maybe too dumb
To see its worth in productivity

Oh well, let us howl like the dog now
And back to work

keep moving

Waiting for the postman
Always
Waiting for the next
Development
Always
I step out to the boxes
Can still smell his cologne
Nothing much today
The small expenses
Of living

We pay them and move on
If we can't pay them
They fine us a little
And we pay on that
And move on
We don't much care
Anymore
We just pay
And try to move on
Here, take this
And please, leave us alone

I just absorb the news
Bad or good
Brush it off and move on
I guess the thing you learn
Is there is no news
Nothing new under the sun
Only life and death right?
And all is vanity
And yet everything is constantly new
A ringing phone

A knock at the door
An afternoon storm
Sirens circling the block
Ideas popping in my head
Water boiling on the stove

sunday

Today we have done one thing and another
But not much
Laid around quite a bit
In front of the fan
Moaning and groaning
Napping and not napping
Thinking and not thinking
Talking a little
Watching tv and eating in bed
Sipping cool drinks
A dog day all the way
And now it's night and cooled down a bit
I sit here in front of the bright screen
And she is down for the evening
Still half clothed asleep on the bed

Tomorrow I take my mother to a hospital
To have a biopsy, a lump in her breast
She discovered last week while we were
Away in New York doing the play
I can only hope and pray it's not serious
Coming up on the first anniversary
Of my dad's death

It's hard to believe my dad is dead
In many ways I guess I don't
I guess I'm in denial
Or so I've thought
Because I never felt
That I properly grieved
And this I suppose because I don't know how
And because at the time of the funeral
I felt that I needed to keep it together

For my mother and family
But mainly, as I say
Because I don't know how
Oh, I know how one grieves
I have helped people in their grieving
But I don't know how to grieve
Not for my father

can man arrested

The KPD got their can man
This morning making his rounds to the dumpsters
The can man was stopped and questioned
By a police officer on bike patrol
I watched this from the window
And then as I walked the dog in back
Of the gravel parking lot
The police officer was off his bike
Standing by the can man who stood slack
Beside his big bag of cans
I saw him there in his grimy old clothes
Lift his long arms a little from his sides
Open palmed in an expression
Of what? why?
And then still standing and waiting
A squad car pulled up
And another officer got out
Then another squad car
And another uniform
One of them pulled the can man's arms
Behind him and put the cuffs on
Then they put on their plastic gloves
And searched his pockets
Finding nothing, not even keys
Totally empty pockets they left pulled out
Then they led him over and put him in the back
Of one of the cars and drove him off

One of the other officers carried
The can man's bag of possessions
Over to the dumpster
When he realized it was too big to push
Through the open door

He considered throwing it over the top
But that would've been some work
So he just drug it to the edge
Of the parking lot and pushed it
Into the hedge behind a parked car
Then they stood around awhile chatting
After about ten minutes one got back
In his car and drove off
The bicycle cop got on his bike
And pedaled down to the next parking lot
Where he sat poised at the entrance
Like a gigantic hood ornament

happy birthday brother

The day before his birthday
And my brother lets me know
"Yeah and I don't want to go anywhere"

And tonight, I don't even want to step outside
To see the fireworks myself
I'd rather just stay in here

I'm tired and I have to get up early
Thought about going down for a drink
At the bar
But it always turns late
And the next day's wasted
I'll do it anyway
But not tonight

Maybe I'll buy him a lamp for his desk
I saw today that he could use a lamp
A good desk lamp with a neck you can stretch
But then awhile ago I went to the shelf
And found his book
Opened it to a couple of lines

The scarecrow lifts
his disheveled
hat and coat
off the drought stalk
and walks away

Shaken from the tree
the wind chimes
flutter their wings

Who has a pocket
for the sea?

And on the opposite page
An even shorter one called

Meditation

a snowflake
could fall
a long way
through silence,
before it ever
makes a sound

And I think, how lovely
And that either of them
Enlarged on some nice paper
And framed to hang
Maybe near his desk but maybe not
Maybe in his bedroom where
All the boxes of baseball cards
Are still stacked and stored
And boxes of books still sit
Holding up the years around the bed
Would help make the whole room
The great poem that it is
Maybe
Yeah
Happy birthday, brother

september

September and the mornings are cooler
A lovely thing after the long hot summer
In East Tennessee there's usually a particular day
When the seasons make their change
A clarity you can feel in your bones
And maybe when you're outside walking
The dog or going to work some secret
Subtle smell from your childhood slips
Its way through the years of mess of
Polluted air and the insane wreck of urban
Repair to sweep you away for a moment
If you're smart you'll stop everything right then
And trace it back as far as you can

The water ran dirty then chalky
In our apartment this morning
I called the landlord just to let him know
Said I figured they were working
On the pipes somewhere and it would
Clear up as the day went on
He said he'd get by when he could to
Check it out but it was okay by tonight
And we had water in the refrigerator
We could use for coffee this morning

The small problems of living
But down in the low country
Of Louisiana and Mississippi
They got nothing but dirty water now
Right up to their necks and beyond
'Six feet of water in the streets of Evangeline'
And none to drink
No refrigerator no kitchen no house

Maybe no town no city no more
Count your blessings brothers and sisters
Things are made to come apart
We were born to die

Louisiana, Louisiana
They're tryin' to wash us away
They're tryin' to wash us away

hurricanes

I once stayed in a beach house
With a few cousins
During a hurricane
They were from the coast and I
Just a foolish interloper
Drifted down from the hills
To the low country of Carolina
My mother and her sisters had wisely
Gone on inland to higher ground
And continued to call and plead with us
To do the same until the phones went out
But we stupidly stayed on observing
The peculiar phenomenon at close range
The inner doors of the house tightening shut
From external wind pressure
The trees outside bent backwards
Daylight turning into a theater of the absurd
The electrical lines dancing in sparks
One thing and another flying by
And the sea roiling and gnarling up
Into an angry monster
At one point I asked my only
Somewhat wiser cousin
What would it be like?
He a man of the sea
And looking out the strained windows
That threatened to explode in our faces
At any moment
Said, it will be so loud that
It'll be like silence
And it'll roll right over us and take us away
I've never forgotten this
We were lucky then

The monster subsided to a tropical storm
That passed with the night
And we were spared

The following day I made promises
To my distraught mother
Who had grown up in the low country
With the death and devastation
Of hurricanes
That I would not torment her like that again
That I would not do this again
And eventually we all
More or less went on with our vacation

But still it will come
We know it will come
In the form of one monster or another
And take us away
Death, so loud it will be like silence
Will blow right through us
Turn us inside out
And we won't know a thing
Life has no answer for death
Does it?
No pocket for the sea

can man's statement

Yesterday I talked to a friend
In the district attorney's office
Who gave me the lowdown
On the can man's arrest
Said the police took him in
For having an 'open container'
He must have found an
Unopened beer in the dumpster
And popped it and was drinking it
When the cop came by
Funny thing, my friend said
When the judge booked him for
Open container the can man said
I don't see how you can drink it if it ain't open

who's buying who

I don't know who's buying what anymore
I don't know who's buying who
I can't keep up with that crap anymore
There's a world out there
Teetering between madness and survival
Sometimes all I can do to help
Is go mad myself
Can you follow me?
Maybe not
And I can't blame you
But what are you doing?
Where are you going?
Better to go mad and say
What you think
Than to sit and stew
In a brew of lies and half truths
Boiling in a slow meltdown
We've got enough human robots now
Enough human jukeboxes
Enough non-human politicians
Non-human teachers and preachers
Find another line of work
Or get real
Try losing an election
By telling the truth
Invite your constituency
To vote you out
And replace you with a robot
Tell them who owns the robot
And who owns them
Tell them the truth
Don't be afraid to lose
Or to live

buy this

October 4th and the rent past due
Child support and a slew of other bills
No work til the weekend
And it won't pay much
Then no work til the end of the month
I've got lots to do
But nothing pays
Something's got to give
What can I sell?
But all I want to do
Is make a new record
Tour Europe again in the spring
Get the house on the mountain built
And write this poem

bloodshot

October 5 and cooling down
Took my mother for chemo yesterday
Bless her heart
Today I take her back for a 'blood shot'
Makes me think of Blood Shot Records
In Chicago
I had a song on one of their compilations
Wonder what happened to them?
They're still around
I don't guess they're wondering what
Happened to me
I'm still here in East Tennessee wailing away
On a few songs and scratching out
Some poems
Checking out the morning sun cutting
Sideways through the trees
The autumn light coming into this part
Of the world where it all began
Where it all began for me mom
Where all that music began that
Blood Shot was so taken with
Do they even know the history here
Much less what's happening now?
It all goes to hell so fast
But we're hanging on
Me and mom
The music

bird clock

The only clock in here
Is this big round bird clock
Hanging on the wall
Above me
Charlie gave it to me
When I lived at his place
The great horned owl is at 12 o'clock high
The little house wren at 6
A northern cardinal at 3 o'clock
And the belted kingfisher at 9
And a bird for every number between
But the mockingbird is number 1
After so many moves and re-settings
And back and forth for daylight savings
The birds have gotten a little confused
With the numbers and who knows
What bird might sing out
At what hour now
And the songs have changed some too
For all I know some of the birds have flown
This was never home to some of them anyway
They might have gone back to Charlie's
Or maybe the place on 12th with the old trees
They may have just passed on
I mean, in one way or another
And sometimes I think
I mean, sometimes it occurs to me
That all of them are the mocker
That it's him now
Singing and squawking and cooing
Trilling and chirping
No matter what time or whose song
I think it's the mockingbird

holding the morning

It's true that sometimes
I would hold the morning
And not let it go
Like a lover or some sleepy dream
You want to doze off to again
I would stay there and make it
All things for myself
For much longer than just a morning
That is if I could hold time like that
If I could stop the world
And make it stay like that
I recall crazy wonderful nights
When I hated to see the dawn arrive
When the dark was too good
Too lovely in its miraculous shroud
And the revelry and joy so grand
I wanted it to go on and on
And if each of us had such possession
We would be scattered through our days
Through our years like clips of film
Playing over and over again
Some never leaving a party
Others a kiss
Others continually rushing ahead
To a blissful rendezvous
Or waiting and watching into the eyes
Of their only vision
Hanging on to what we love the best
Unwilling to leave those moments
To gamble on anything being better
Perhaps we are already much like this
Perhaps we are just like this

why do I live (or) all that water

Why do I live the life I live?
Because it's so good
A guitar leaning over there
To be picked up anytime
Acoustic or electric
Just waiting to come alive!
And songs to sing and poems to write
And shelves of books to read
So many I've yet to open
And this magic screen
That locates everything
And helps my thoughts to flow
And all my files!
Something new every day
And the weather!
The incredible unpredictable weather
Even the news
The Times and the times
And I have shows to play
I have to hurry up and book some shows
And I have to play some shows
I have to go out and do it!
And I have to wash the dishes
And straighten up around here
And I'll make the bed
That magic bed where we make love
And the good coffee
Pretty much the first thing
Every morning
Unless I'm already going
Already shaping words
If not the world
With my mind

And my hands
Maybe a dream
A dream that comes through
From sleep
That passes over
Into this world
Into words
And you know it belongs to you
Yours to declare
To contemplate
To revisit
To let go
This is my life
And of course I want to live it
Art and Love, my baby says
Art and Love, I say too
That's how we live it
The day is for doing and loving
And of course I want to live it
I don't want to trade it
It's my soul
It's what I'm working on
I'm not envious of any other
I just want to shake it up
And take it outside
Down the streets
And into the market place
Push the city limits a little
And take it out to the wilds
And up to the hills
Up to the holy mountain
And down to the sea
Down to the blood and the tides

And wash all your sins
And see what you can gather
From all that water
All that water flowing
Through your hands
Through your mind and body
All that water here in this life
Where we live it

flutter off

Indian summer I'd say
50 degrees or better
And the sun strolling through
Still coming
Even as we know
It's fixing to turn a corner
And leave town
The big maple across the street
In full glory now
A heavy golden yellow
And coming slowly down
Slow and steady
Covering the ground already
And I'm alone behind the glass
Keeping an eye on it all
As if it wouldn't take place otherwise
But of course only this little exercise
Wouldn't take place otherwise
The rest is in the cards
It's on the slate
Destined to go down
Out of my hands

There they go again
A little breeze kicking up
And they flutter away
The clock is ticking on us all
What have we got?
Hard to say
Will we make it to May?
Another spring?
Another birthday?
Another dream or two

In the arms of a lover?
Another song on the radio
Passing by in another car?
Another blink of the eye
And that chilly wind
Will be at our back
Cutting us loose from all we know
Are you ready to turn colors
And flutter away?

death

In the face of it
People do funny things
Kill other people certainly
Sometimes just freeze up
Panic and shake right on down
Through death's door
Or crawl so far inside
They don't even know
They're alive anymore
Until they're not
But then, some get real smart, you know?
A lucid moment if not an epiphany
Sometimes a sort of rupture of the heart
And start acting abnormal as if possessed
Some ecstatic humor or erratic behavior
Maybe some message or mission
Making it difficult for the rest of us
To go about our business
You know?
By the way, what is your business?
I imagine old Saint Pete at the golden gate
Checking IDs
"Just state your business please"

99%

The wind howls hard and cold
Outside the window
Like a choir of Chihuahuas
Running up and down the street
The leaves flying sideways
Like cars blowing by
Trees bent to the last of November
No reason to be out there
We've got some heat in here
Not a lot in the cupboard
But a little food in the fridge
Tomorrow is Thanksgiving
So let us be thankful
You know, glad to be alive
Count your blessings
Yeah, I'm in pretty good health
As far as I can tell
No pains no complaints
Not much money
No health insurance
But when it gets right down to it
I'm probably better off than 99%
Of the rest of the world
I've got a lovely daughter
Who loves and respects me
And she's here visiting now
I've got a beautiful young girlfriend
Who would like to spend the rest
Of her life with me
Who shares our elegant poverty
As though we were king and queen
I have some good friends
Who have stuck with me over the years

Just knowing all this helps
As the days slide by unresolved

But still somewhere
Out there in that icy breeze
In that brutal world that doesn't care
Somewhere out there
I'm blowing wild like a leaf
Somewhere with that other 99
I gnash and weep and wail
I howl like a dog
Like a madman falling down the street
I plot and scheme and I scream
And reach my hands up as far
As I can into the tree
And I grab for all I can hold
And shake and shake and shake

everything you do will be forgotten

"What will become of the world when you leave?
No matter what happens, no trace of now will remain."
                                        -Arthur Rimbaud

It would appear as though every generation lasts
Just long enough to raise its blossomed head above
The dust and rust of transience to see with some
Dull clarity the folly and birthright of their blindness
Only then to fall back into the shimmering folds
And disappear
Their offering little forged in the sink of time
Everything you do will be forgotten
Just figure on that
All is gone even as it goes
The love, the endeavor, the works
The Alamo will be forgotten
Just like Rimbaud, Shakespeare, Rasputin
Willy Mays, Einstein, Lincoln
It all passes, even heaven and earth
Remember?
And this the Age of Impermanence
As if there was ever another
The Nuclear Age
And what has the Bomb given us
But a new awareness of impermanence
And believe me, I'm not a pessimist
I see it all as a call to love and care
And endeavor to persevere
I take some pride in our great run
Even as I see us veering off the curve
If we're not careful
And still we're driven
By notions of immortality

Whatever that might be
By Heaven and Art and Forever
I like all those guys
Whoever they are
But as Burroughs said
We are here to go
Here to go
Born to die
And be gone
Born to forget
And be forgotten

So, what do you want to do?
Have a drink?
No?
Make love to someone?
Make a lot of money?
Sit and watch the clouds play in the sun?
Go downtown and start feeding the hungry?
Maybe just try and take it easy
You know, I'm starting to like you

a tiger behind the 8 ball

Last night I dreamed of tigers
A couple of tigers that I befriended
It was tricky but it worked out
And I think it was because of the good love
We shared before going to sleep
Not just the lovemaking
Which was wonderful
But the strength and goodness I felt
In the love all day

She wants to get married
It never leaves her mind now for long
Things'll be going just fine like yesterday
Shooting some 8 ball at the Branch
Laughing and having an afternoon beer
And all of a sudden she'll ask me to marry her
Right away I'm behind the 8 ball again
Sliding this way and that
Making combinations of excuses
And scratching all over the place
And she's bummed, game over

I guess the biggest thing is having kids
I'll be 54 in May
And have a daughter nearly grown
I can easily say my daughter's the best thing
That ever happened to me
But to go through it all again now
Now when I've finally got turned around
And settled into my ways?

Agh- fuck me
No balls that's all

And no great love in my heart
I know

My artist buddy Rocket says
You'll be like Picasso pushing a baby carriage
When you're 60

Maybe
She's 30 years younger than me
I guess I shouldn't complain
And I won't
Another course I signed on for

Just rack'em up
And crack'em up again

the game

We were sitting in Li Po's
In Chinatown, San Francisco
Me and Karly and Phil Cousineau
And Kevin from the Green Apple Bookstore
All having nice cold beers and talking
I was told it was an old Kerouac hangout
Now some Chinese mafia joint
Fairly calm and unadorned
At least not a tourist shop
Selling nothing but beer and booze
And a vague hospitality
We wandered through to a back room
And big corner booth a world away from the street
It felt wonderful
Like I was on a ship out to sea
And happy in a glorious daze
Just to relax between whatever else
We had to do and sip on a cold brew
It was suggested that we each write
Something down on paper
A line or two, a game
Where we all compare them later
It was more than I wanted to think about
But did when I saw that everyone was into it
If only just to pass the time at sea
And yes, let us row ourselves out
To that great ship and...
Suddenly it was discovered
We were late to be somewhere and
Had to swallow down those beers and
Hustle back out to the street and
All the spectacle of lights and people
And up a Chinatown hill to somewhere

To catch back up with time

The steam off the anchor fed the red light
and lifted like a thousand years of Chinese
history lapping in to the western lip

I found it by chance a year later
Lost in a little tool box
In Knoxville
Maybe that was the game

cold mountain

Who can break the snares of the world
and sit with me among the white clouds?   -Han Shan

From Cold Mountain
To Gold Mountain they came
I saw the great migration
In a dream
I saw the terrible distance
The great fall of humanity
Like the earth spinning backwards
Coming into view from above
And the procession moving us all
We all have our own lives to behold
The days the nights
The memories
Though mostly forgotten
We have our magic connection
Our melancholia
Our moments of passion
And compassion
Our good luck and bad
But do you know when
You came closest to godhead?
When you came closest to devil?
From Cold Mountain to Gold Mountain
The journey of a billion souls
Of a mighty race
They came from east to west
From west to east
They came and they came
We all arrived
But who can make the journey back
From Gold Mountain to Cold Mountain?

dream

I heard a voice in a dream
When you turn 54
You are more or less alone
They were speaking to someone younger
Unaware that I was even there, I guess
It was my dream after all
And I saw waves crashing
On just the other side of the beach house
Giant waves maybe 20 feet high
Though it was otherwise calm
And the girl I was with
My high school sweetheart
We were hungry and in some beach town
With nowhere to stay
We were in the side yard of a beach house
That belonged to someone else
We had secretly slept there
between the houses
And I saw giant waves crashing
Just beneath the porches
People came down where we slept
And sat near us eating and we got up
They gave us a bag that had food in it
But it was beef that we didn't eat
And I thought to walk to the sea
To get closer
But the path was thick with briers
in that direction
And I turned back for then
Thinking we need to talk with these people
And establish where we are
My girlfriend and the other girl with us
Were already sitting and talking with them

It was difficult for me to come around
To where they were
Chairs and benches were in the way
That's when I heard one of them say it
And it seemed true to me then
That I was separated and alone and getting older
Caught between briers and a raging sea
And somewhere I wasn't supposed to be

take that ride

It's a hard thing baby
I'm not sure you want to hear it
I'm not sure death is going to teach us
How to live properly
But it's going to try
You'll see them all fall away
Every face every heart
Heaven and earth if you could last that long
Meantime there'll be plenty
To get caught up in
I guess we need these screens
Between us and all the pain
We all have to find our level of denial
Those who work to make it better
Can only make it a little better
Can only handle it a little more
It's a hard thing baby
I'm not sure death is going to teach us
How to love properly
But it's going to try
Do you really want to take that ride
With me?

a vacant lot

No poetry this morning
The voices of the ages have curled back
Beneath the covers of time
And left me here in chilly silence

Let's not disturb them
Let the ethers settle
A small respite from the constant call
Upon their attentions

Maybe sleep will fall back over us
Like the rain against the window
The slush of cars pushing by on the street
Taking us away

That old sunny trail

A sunny day
About 20 degrees I believe
Late December
What do you expect?
Winding down another year
All these years
That have come and gone
Maybe a few more
Before we all come and go
Before I come and go
Wonder where I'll be going next?
I haven't really heard for sure
Hard to get good information around here
And to think all these people
Arguing and suing and warring
Over what little they do know

Yeah, *I used to be a rambler*
A child of the sun
Wherever I was going then
I guess I'll be picking back up
On that old sunny trail before long
Following it on over the hill

day 1

The chilly wind blows against the old window
The temp has dropped to its knees

We sit with no plan whatsoever
As the new year stretches into day 1

And still we say there are things to finish
Life remains unfinished

And so it will be
Accept this resolutely we suggest

But this will never do
We must finish one thing and another

Then go, though we don't know
Where when why

Cry if you like
I'm trying to catch a cold

Actually I'm catching a cold
Without trying

While trying to do something else
Trying to finish one year

And begin another
Trying to drink my third glass of water

Let us flush ourselves clean
Let us begin again

Our futures are full of new fluidities
New releases and epic moves

Yes, and old debts, old habits
Serious doubts

Make it sound pretty
You old curmudgeon

Don't hide the gentle side
Don't hide your light under a mountainside

Is this the year we move the mountain?
Day one glass four

idiocy suffering hope

Every once in a while
You have to lift up a prayer
For the human race
Even if it's just to say *please*!
Yeah, a little prayer
For the whole lousy lot of them
And not because you necessarily
Believe in God almighty
Or anyone hearing your prayer
But somehow you reach out anyway
Somehow you lift up a little
Gesture to the broader body
Probably out of desperation
Out of the pain you feel
For all the suffering
And for all the idiocy going down
Yeah maybe that's it
All the suffering and all the idiocy
Going down out there and in here
In my life my world
My little providence among the ruins
The ruins that gather before we die
And follow every human being
The whole bag of worms that we are
We're all covered in blood and shit
We just have to turn and lift together
And strive to sing a new song
Yeah, and what good does it do?
Maybe nothing
Maybe no good at all
But at least you cried out
Your heart took a turn
For a moment

And was lifted
If not the burden of the world
I've heard there's new science
That says even this makes a difference
That the whole is effected by
The smaller parts in our thoughts
That we're all connected
In ways we haven't generally known
More like a wave than a mountain
It's hard to understand
It's hard to know
We can't know
We just hope

marked

A tangle of vines across the window
The cold morning air trembling at the glass
The dog is here
Old chunks of wood laid flat for tables
My daughter asleep in the next room
I saw myself in the mirror earlier
Just after waking from dreams
The bump on my head
The place I've come to live
The years of this
Being on the outside
I had thought myself the good guy
I had spiritual leanings
A world vision that included everyone
I intended to be part of the solution
Who knows, that could be true yet
But now, I see that I'm marked
That I've sinned every sin
Again and again
And my path has always been near the edge
Of darkness

But then a redbird on a low branch outside
A train whistle across town
People moving along the sidewalks

a winter garden

This new record will be out by early spring
I think I'll call it Empire
It'll have a European theme
A huge nude on the cover
With my name and the title
This should be somehow simpatico
With the social poetics of the people
When we go back to the UK in May
This book will probably be ready too
And back from the printers when I return
By then I'm thinking one of those hat acts
In Nashville will have had the good sense
To cover a song of mine
There should be some money in the pipeline
Advanced to me
I've got my own publishing now
Rich Mountain Bound
100%
I can use that cash to finish the cabin
Up in the mountains
Put a sod roof on
A skylight or two
Pay for the doors and windows
Gather what wood I can in my spare time
Put back some coffee and liquor
Some can goods and good books
Be all tucked in by first snowfall
Tell the rest of the world to go to hell

mozart's little afternoon drive

Thing is if I can write something here
I can excuse myself for countless other things
I didn't do that need done
Yeah, maybe that's what it becomes
A windshield to the world through which I see
But to otherwise shield me
From the onslaught of responsibility
Sad, eh?
Yeah, tell that to Mozart
Mozart was telling that to me
I was telling Mozart that I'm no Mozart
And he's no Jesus, who neither toils nor spins
And all those lilies of the valley
All those lovely clouds floating by
That lovely sky never ceasing
Always in motion
Every atom assuming us all
And I'm just afraid you won't be able to be
All things to all cows under the sun buster brown
And you won't be no Mozart or no good lord Jesus
But it's all in what you choose and how
You see
So, what's it going to be maestro?

indian giver

When I was a kid we played a lot
Of cowboys and Indians
Not so many cops and robbers
The romance of the city
Didn't stack up
To the wild west in those early days
Sometimes it was just cowboys and cowboys
And sometimes you're the bad guy
But most times it was cowboys and Indians
Though sometimes there weren't any Indians
We were all cowboys just shooting at Indians
The Indians were invisible like ghosts or spirits
They became part of the rocks and trees
But they were out there somewhere
To play an Indian was like playing
A bad guy only different
A bad guy did something bad
But an Indian was just an Indian
Whatever that was
And what that was
Was wild
Indians were wild
A wild Indian
And if you played an Indian
You could be as wild as you wanted
I guess it was only a matter of time
Before I preferred being an Indian
Instead of a cowboy
Everyone wanted to be a cowboy
And I was still a cowboy
But I had drifted over to the wilder side
After a while it just suited me better

I would rather be Huck Finn than Tom Sawyer
I would rather be Tarzan than the great white hunter
There was a wilder dignity
To being an Indian
You were automatically a warrior
Almost extraterrestrial but very much of the earth
And somewhere in there
I came to a new understanding
Of *Indian givers*
Who my brothers and the boys
In the neighborhood
Always called someone who
Gave you something then took it back
I was just a kid
But I thought the Indians were the givers
I thought it meant
You couldn't trust an Indian
To stick to his deal
That he would give you something
Then steal it back
That's what I thought
And I don't doubt
That a/A lot of people
Still think that's what it means
But think again Kemosabe

half of what I say is meaning less

And now I've fought with my father
Argued and cursed and threatened violence
I've pushed every emotional button he has
Til he spit fury at me
I was doing it out of some kind of hurt
Though I don't know what
But I know I hurt him
I upset him terribly
I threw all his shortcomings up in his face
I made him hate himself by hating me
That's what I was going for
Whether I knew it or not
And all over some lawnmower
And filling it back up with gas
Good thing it was only a dream
But it was just as real
And I feel just as bad
Waking in the dark
Wanting to tell him how
Sorry I am

before the dawn

Can't sleep
Still the middle of the night I guess
I'm not looking for a clock
I hear trains clanging over
Rails a mile away
I hear a mockingbird working
The graveyard shift
I wake up and worry
Worry about debts I owe
Things I've left undone
The love I don't give
The regrets, I guess
I wake up and can't go back to sleep
Sometimes I read
But the bedside lamp may wake her too
And she needs her sleep
Before the alarm goes off
So I come in here

I've already got a list of to do's for the day
Fill out a non-custodial parental form
For my daughter's college
Mail books and cds
Try to do some promotion for this show
On wednesday
Contact a string of people
About one thing and another
Including Europe
Just a few more shows in Ireland
And we should break even
Stuff like that
I mean, that's the good stuff

But it's nice
Nice to hear the night birds sing
A concert not many take in
And yet encore after encore
Night after night
Nice to feel the quiet
Such as it is
And watch the sky ease itself
Through a prism of changes
Cutting shapes through curtains and blinds
Across ceiling and walls
Like the dreams you left back in bed
Like the people and places you've known
In your life
All your life
Coming to this night

my cousin freddie's house

The nature and meaning of existence?

Yeah, that's a tough one
I saw the best minds of my generation
Just let that one go

Just the mention of it either
Puts them off or sends them off
Expounding into theory
Often with great eloquence
And blossoming confidence
As if they were giving you directions
To their cousin Freddie's house

For some it's all a matter of information

"When we get the right information,
Then we'll know."

Right, but wrong
I don't think so
Not quite, but then
I can't explain
Let me just say
You're not going to get
The right information
Not now not ever
That's not the nature of the deal
There'll always be more information
More incoming
And yes gather it up
Add it up
Apply it well

All that
And leave behind
Or reinterpret
Old ideas
Theories
Knowledge

That's the process
That's living
But it's not going to sum up
To a nice equation for you
No, it's a numberless song we sing
You don't really corner it with facts
It's a flow a wave
Not a place at all
Except in a way of speaking
You can't really
Put your finger in the river
In the same place twice
Or as Corso said
In the same place once
Because it's not there
Because you're not there

So
Might as well let go
All those big time
Conceptions that don't
Add up to the sky

We exist in unknowing
Unknowing is the nature
Unknown is the meaning

That's what keeps Science going
And Religion alive
And Art happening

Do you want to figure it?
Or stand in awe of it?
Or reveal it?

Well, all the above, of course
Me too
So look, meet me at my cousin Freddie's
It's easy to find
See you there

village idiot

You realize of course
I have to keep writing this down

Not because it's something
You need to see

No, it's hard to say
What you need to see

It's just something
I have to deal with

Something I need to see
But we all bear witness

And you may be
Working it out for yourself

I'm sure most by now
Have their rationale in harness

Their blinders locked down
And the doctor's horse in step

Most of the ones
I've known anyway

Who probably aren't that far
From where I sit this minute

This good morning in this
Rented apartment here in this

Town where I was born and raised
Most probably have their house and yard

Claimed and cut out among
The other houses and yards

Their cars parked exactly where
They always park them

Their two and a half kids
Off to their own houses and cars

And kids by now
And they into the morning routines

Of their livelihoods
Their affirmations and denials

You see, not unlike me at all
Only, they may have bought something

I would never afford
Something they can't even name

And won't slow down for a second
To recognize

Not for the love of their soul
Or any other light

Except to keep
Choking it down

Shifting whatever parameters
Are necessary as it's

Parroted down to them
Never using their overeducated brains

To figure out a fucking thing
Besides pushing a few beans

Around the board
I think they've already turned

The page on all this
Don't you?

If not closed the book

terry

I had a dream of my dead friend
He visited me in an afternoon nap
There he was bigger than life
Bigger than me as I seemed to be sitting
Next to him with my head
Only about waist high looking up
I was going to draw something on his arm
With an ink pen
I thought to draw a heart
With an arrow through it
I saw and felt his white skin
But then he showed me
A bracelet around his hand and wrist
Where something was already drawn
It was in layers of black and white
One layer showing through the other
Making an intricate pattern
Of something I couldn't entirely make out
Then he showed me the sunglasses
That he was wearing
He handed them to me to look through
They not only had the two main
Lenses that cover the eyes
But also other smaller lenses to either side
And all around the edges
Like little doors and windows
That further blocked out light
I held them to my eyes
Long enough to look through them
And said to him
It's always night when you wear these
He smiled the sweetest deepest smile
And nodded but never said a thing

lewis and clark

We never did what we set out to do
Did we?

Not quite, eh?
Not by a long shot

Well, we set out
The rest was pretty much a dream anyway

A loose agenda of ambition and curiosity
Not unlike Lewis and Clark

But comes a time
When the river splits

And you have to make a choice
Unless you set up camp there

And cash in all your chips
I suppose there was always talk

Of cashing in the chips
You just never thought this is it

Oh where is my Muse?
My great lost Sea?

I have my Indian princess

crazy horse

You know, it's true
At times
I have lamented
Not being
Some famous artist
Not being more
Renowned and compensated
Yes, but
It's as though the good lord
Knew I might
Over indulge myself
And dull my edge
Squander my passion
Make less of a gift
And so, I am kept here
With the bees
Buzzing in my ear
And the wind in my face
My welfare unclear
My purpose
In constant question

They say Crazy Horse
Was the Lakota Sioux's
Greatest warrior
A mighty chief
A fearless general
On the field of battle
Never in fact
Was he defeated
He sat within rifle range
Of the 7th Cavalry
Smoking his pipe

Or rode circles around them
Taunting and singing
Inviting them to shoot him
And much as they tried
They never could
No, Crazy Horse
The great Sioux warrior
Hero of countless battles
And skirmishes
Including the real showdown
Of brains and courage
Little Big Horn
Was never defeated in battle
But Crazy Horse
Never wore
The great headdress
And all the feathers
And symbols
Of a Sioux chieftain
He was always to dress
Like a young warrior
Lean and bare
As his vision had instructed
A small stone behind his ear
Would protect him
He would have no fear
Of his enemies

It was only under the white flag
That they would finally entice him
To come forward to the fort
To powwow with the great white chiefs
Sitting Bull had gone on

With the people to Canada
While Crazy Horse stayed behind
With the sacred land
But once he had entered the fort
Slowly and nobly
On his proud pony
A great man
Who would honor
The truce
Of the white man flag
It was easy then for the many
To lay hands upon him
And hold him down
And murder him

Who will pray with me this day?
Who will take the vision quest
To see where it leads and what it asks?
Who will fight a different war?

windmills

Hard to believe the world has come this far
Where old poets are now dead
Where enchanted woods and fields of youth
Are subdivisions and urban sprawl
But still birds sing
Looking out the window at changeling March
We have given the days names
And drawn pictures on the stars
We are well possessed of time
And still the birds sing
And still the old wild king
Rides out against the night
And rails his rag at the spectral heavens
Clashing with phantoms where convened
All weapons archaic and useless
Making music making war
Whirling in air and who for?
And who asks?

a fine little ritual

What a fine little ritual, she said
Untying the curtains and pulling them together
Closing out the fast closing light of evening
She switches on a lamp
The screened windows still open
And stray lines of conversation coming
Through from the sidewalk

The ritual of what goes on
Behind the curtain behind the screen
We hear voices from beyond
A voice seeps out from within
And she does a little dance
On the way to my arms
Bodies in abiding motion
Just like the stars
Just like atoms dancing
Unto ourselves
Assuming us all through a veil

Well, let me just sum up here
Find a nice ribbon and make a bow
Give it a name
And go do something else
Of course I could just say
It's all been said before
And nothing much to add
I could fold it over now
Where it will soon fold over anyway
Back into the folds
And what good would it do to say more?
It's as though we're being punished
For all our abuses of the language

With the babble we now endure
Nothing is said clearly
People have quit looking for clarity
Wouldn't know what it was if it bit them
On the nose

Here, come closer

upstairs

There's a guy upstairs blows a sax
Young fellow from out of town
Going to the university I guess
Probably a student of their celebrated
Jazz department
I don't know
But he plays real good
A fine full bodied tone
That only comes to me subdued
Through windows and trees
And three floors
He always plays low
Laidback soulful lines
Probably not wanting to disturb
Other tenants any more than necessary
And this suits me fine
So now in these late afternoons
And early evenings
When the smooth notes
And melodic phrases
Begin to rise
To the threshold of my ear
Like a sublime dream recurring
It's like a mantra that brings me back
To the here and now
Where I am forever connected
To this room and these days
These long gone Knoxville days

live and not lern
          (for Smokn' Dave and the Premo Dopes)

There was a time when the gods walked the earth
At least in Fort Sanders
Where the mockingbird was king
And there was fresh dew on the ruins
Naked in the Fort they sat on porches
Or spied themselves from sidewalks
Passing freely from one body to another
They became whoever
They could appear at the top of the stairs
They could walk down the middle of the street
They could be naked with their clothes on
Maybe that's what made them gods
Or birds or angels
As they became everything
And every voice

Of course, the gods didn't care
That's the trouble with angels
You never know what they're thinking
They get on your nerves
They bring the tail out in you
You never know what you got
Til you're dead

And from a lonely hill of old houses
They reached out to Hollywood to Africa
To Emerald City
From a spot on the lung
To a spot on the sun
They donned the world and became human
They became soldier boys and rock stars
Carnies and French monkeys

Merry-go-rounds and body bags
And whores and ambassadors
And great conversationalists
A few suicides, a few Lucifers
A few went straight to heaven
On cracks of light in wedding songs
But there they were, going home

Afterwards, others came and went
Plugging into systems better
Bringing down more highlights
But that shit don't matter
The earth had been rolled and walked upon
The thought had been thought
A song was sung and was echoing yet
If only they had known
They were alive

Everyone was shocked at the death of Mockingbird
Even the ones who pulled the trigger
Long buried now beneath older ruins
Somewhere in the highland forest
Deep beneath the laurels
Now it's only a myth, as they say
And no one believes that gods could walk
Or talk, much less sing in trees
Or on porches or in your dreams
All of a sudden everybody's a realist

Still, those lost anthems come to us
As we doze in the daze of hazy seasons
Or whistle absently past gnarled magnolias
On the way to the beer store
Or glimpse the aura of certain houses
As people come and go

spring

April and the sun
Poking out between showers
People out walking dogs
In the grass to do their business
Me, I'm all about it
Sober as most judges
Awake and watching
I hear the morning dove coo
Between a swoosh of cars
I welcome the day
You are never too old
To be what you might have been
Someone said

But, Spring is here! Eucharis told Rimbaud
In a budding grove, in a blooming stand of violets
But Rimbaud saw that nobody really cares
He said since the Flood it's been nothing
But business as usual all over again
So you might as well bring back the waters
Bring back the floods!
Only next time it'll be fire
It'll be worse
At least that's what I heard

Yes, but I am an old paradoxical
Calling for another walk into the nether
Just as the dark clouds are gathering
And let us pretend we might catch a thunderbolt
And discover that power that darkness that light
That drove young Arthur into the ether
Into two directions at once singing!

Epilogue

Prelude to a New Season

what was I thinking

I'm not sure what I'm doing
Or what I was thinking

When I drifted away
And disappeared

I just wasn't drawn to it
Enough I guess

A lack of drive
Plain and simple

A lack of ambition
To follow through

To be a world shaker
Scene maker heart breaker

But look
Like the old Apache

I went to where the fight was good
I got back to the root

The biz was a loser
The scene was busted

Got used up and went backward
Hanging out there

Looked a little desperate to me
I see them hustling it up

They're working hard
Making a scene for themselves

Kings of a happy hour
And it's all good

I'm just a guy who comes in late
And watches from a corner

King of a lost hour
And it's okay

I just don't know what I'm doing
Or what I was thinking

But today I took the dog
For a walk down the street

To a cool little park
In the heart of the neighborhood

And the roses are blooming
And the irises are blooming

And hey Jim! check out your lilacs
You can spread a quilt here brother

And the grass is green
Green as the eyes of God

That's right Walt! and look
Who's holding court

Old Mockingbird is the maestro here
Here where the roots run deep

And the great stones lay
Waiting for me to move them

And there's a new song
For the new season

And I'm singing it

tsunami

The little brown man
Squatting on the hill
Is wiser than all of them
He says it's the god of the deep
Who's come to swallow up
Some people
To fill himself
To satisfy his hunger
He will tell you
The gods have to be satisfied
And listen now
How they laugh
What a fool
They think he is
But the waters
Cover up their laughter
While he sits
On the high ground
Above them
Against all odds
Holding the truth

the road

He was holding a book
A well bound paperback
Bigger than pocket size
The covers were black
And across the front
Written in large letters
Was **THE ROAD**
He had turned it over
To read what was written
On the back
And when he looked again
At the front
He saw images in relief
In the black
Behind the words
Slightly darker shadows
He hadn't noticed before
He studied them a moment
And tilted the book
In the light
There were two images
One larger and appearing
In front of the other
Perhaps people walking
And he reached
With his other hand
To touch them
And feel the relief
Then realized
They were not
Part of the cover
Design at all
But the moisture

From his hand
Holding the book
He moved his fingers
Through the images
And watched them
Change and disappear

the falling snow

The snow was falling in Lexington
It was late November
Karly and I drove up for the weekend
So I could play a couple of nights
With John Prine
At the Lexington Opera House

We were staying in a downtown hotel
A few of blocks away
We had stayed there seven years before
On our first date
I was playing shows then too
And she drove over
From Louisville to meet me

The Opera House has great sound
A wonderful theater with its upper balcony
And little side soapbox balconies
Probably seats a 1000 people
And both nights sold out
The first night went really well
I was up for it
I felt like singing
I hadn't played Lexington in a while
And I had new songs
I never knew when I'd be playing
Another show with John Prine
Never knew if I'd get another invite
He's the master songwriter for a lot of people
And his audiences are the best
For many it's like going to church
To hear him revive their old favorites
That night they opened up to me

And I was leaning in
It felt like I was singing to them
In a dream

Next morning after a late breakfast
Karly and I walked out of the hotel
There was ice on the streets
And three or four inches of snow
They were calling for more
And it was coming down
Big lovely flakes all soft
And dreamy in the icy air
We were slipping and sliding and laughing
Trying to make our way around
Trying to find a little music club
I'd heard about and thought might be
A good place to play a show of my own
If I was lucky enough to get booked that day
I could announce it from the stage that evening
Let them know when you'll be back in town
After awhile we found the club
We knocked but it was closed
We stood looking in a window
Through a crack in a curtain
No luck
And I realized I needed a hat

We walked around but nothing much was open
Stopped in a drugstore but the toboggans
They had were tiny ones for kids
We walked on in the snow
They told us there was a shop
A few blocks away that sold only hats

And we went looking for it
We found it but it was closed
We stood at the big front window
Looking at hundreds of hats
Hanging all over the walls and on racks
And stacked on shelves and tables
Scores of them close enough to touch
But for the cold glass between
Any one of them I would have donned
On my weathered head right then
We walked on and the snow
Swirled around like drunken confetti
There was a tobacco shop open
And we went in
A man behind the counter asked
If he could help us
Do you happen to have any hats, I asked
I've got a hat here somewhere, he said
And he started looking
He asked his daughter to look
And his little granddaughter was there too
I figured they were maybe a family business
Three generations hanging out in the store
On a slow snowy Saturday
The granddaughter asked, Grandpa what
Are you looking for?
A hat, he said
There's a hat that comes with that
Turkish tobacco, he told me
And if I can find it I'll give it to you
He asked his daughter to look up under the counter
She shuffled things around under there
But couldn't find any hat
He said, let me look and slowly
Stooped down on his knees

And pushed his arms up under the counter
Sorting through one thing and another
And then brought forth a tightly folded brown cap
He opened it up and said, it has a little flag on it
A Turkish flag
I took it and pushed it down on my head
Took it off again and adjusted the strap
Then stuck it back on
Yes, I said, thank you very much
He smiled and his daughter
And granddaughter smiled too
We bought a few items
And walked back out in the snow
My cap on tight
She smiled at me in my goofy hat
As we walked by statues of soldiers on horses
And the well kept civic buildings
All floating beneath the falling snow
When she turned and smiled at me again
Her face was illuminated by the sky
By the snow itself
A light that's blinding one moment
And the next gives you perfect clarity
She was the face of youth and beauty
Like the lovely face of all humanity
Looking up and believing
Believing but wanting to believe more
I asked her
Karly, will you marry me?
Really? she said
Yes, I said
Yes, she said
And we kissed
In the falling snow

Notes to the text:

p. 44-45 – *happy birthday brother* – The italicized lines are from the poems A Pocket for the Sea and Meditation by Charles Morris, from the book *A Pocket for the Sea* by Charles Morris, Armadillo Poetry Press, (1998).

p. 46-47 – *september* – The italicized phrases from Randy Newman's song *Louisiana 1927*, Alfred Publishing.

p. 64 – The quote is from Arthur Rimbaud's poem *Youth* in the book *Illuminations*.

p. 70 – The quote is from the *Cold Mountain* poems of Han Shan, Shambhala Publications, Inc.

p. 75 – The italicized lines are from David Blue's song Lady O'Lady from the album *Nice Baby and the Angel* (Asylum Records), Good Friends Music/Benchmark Music - ASCAP.

p. 103 – This poem was written for and originally published as the liner notes for the CD re-issue of Smoking Dave and the Premo Dopes' album *Live and Not Lern*, toddsteed.com.

Cover:

Girl with Flowers
Screen print and book design
by Karly Stribling

RB Morris is a poet and performing songwriter from Knoxville, Tennessee. He has published books of poetry including *Early Fires* (Iris Press) and *The Mockingbird Poems*, as well as music albums including *Spies Lies and Burning Eyes* and *Going Back to the Sky*. He wrote and acted in *The Man Who Lives Here Is Loony*, a one-man play taken from the life and work of writer James Agee, and was instrumental in founding a park dedicated to Agee in the Fort Sanders neighborhood of Knoxville. Morris served as the Jack E. Reese Writer-in-Residence at the University of Tennessee from 2004-2008, and was inducted into the East Tennessee Writers Hall of Fame in 2009. He was Knoxville's first Poet Laureate 2016-2017, and lives in Knoxville.

www.ingramcontent.com/pod-product-compliance
Lightning Source LLC
Chambersburg PA
CBHW020942090426
42736CB00010B/1226